GET ADDICTED to free-motion QUILTING

Go from Simple to Sensational

with *Sheila Sinclair Snyder*

Text copyright © 2013 by Sheila Sinclair Snyder

Photography and Artwork copyright © 2013 by C&T Publishing, Inc.

Publisher: **Amy Marson**

Creative Director: **Gailen Runge**

Art Director: **Kristy Zacharias**

Editor: **Lynn Koolish**

Technical Editors: **Doreen Hazel and Teresa Stroin**

Cover Designer: **April Mostek**

Book Designer: **Rose Wright**

Production Coordinators: **Jessica Jenkins and Rue Flaherty**

Production Editor: **Joanna Burgarino**

Illustrator: **Valyrie Friedman**

Photo Assistant: **Mary Peyton Peppo**

Photography by **Christina Carty-Francis and Diane Pedersen** of C&T Publishing, Inc., unless otherwise noted

Published by C&T Publishing, Inc., P.O. Box 1456, Lafayette, CA 94549

All rights reserved. No part of this work covered by the copyright hereon may be used in any form or reproduced by any means—graphic, electronic, or mechanical, including photocopying, recording, taping, or information storage and retrieval systems—without written permission from the publisher. The copyrights on individual artworks are retained by the artists as noted in *Get Addicted to Free-Motion Quilting*. These designs may be used to make items only for personal use. Donations to nonprofit groups or items for sale or for display only at events require the following credit on a conspicuous label: Designs copyright © 2013 by Sheila Sinclair Snyder from the book *Get Addicted to Free-Motion Quilting* from C&T Publishing, Inc. Permission for all other purposes must be requested in writing from C&T Publishing, Inc.

Attention Commercial Machine Quilters: If your client brings you this book as a source for quilting designs, you may reproduce as many designs as you wish on that client's quilt *only*. If your client does not own this book, the publisher and author encourage you to sell a copy to your client. Contact C&T Publishing (800-284-1114) with your business name and resale number to purchase this book at a special resale price. For clients wishing to use designs from this book, but not willing to purchase a copy, you may reproduce *no more than 10 designs total for commercial purposes.*

Attention Teachers: C&T Publishing, Inc., encourages you to use this book as a text for teaching. Contact us at 800-284-1114 or www.ctpub.com for lesson plans and information about the C&T Creative Troupe.

We take great care to ensure that the information included in our products is accurate and presented in good faith, but no warranty is provided nor are results guaranteed. Having no control over the choices of materials or procedures used, neither the author nor C&T Publishing, Inc., shall have any liability to any person or entity with respect to any loss or damage caused directly or indirectly by the information contained in this book. For your convenience, we post an up-to-date listing of corrections on our website (www.ctpub.com). If a correction is not already noted, please contact our customer service department at ctinfo@ctpub.com or at P.O. Box 1456, Lafayette, CA 94549.

Trademark (™) and registered trademark (®) names are used throughout this book. Rather than use the symbols with every occurrence of a trademark or registered trademark name, we are using the names only in the editorial fashion and to the benefit of the owner, with no intention of infringement.

Library of Congress Cataloging-in-Publication Data

Snyder, Sheila Sinclair.

 Get addicted to free-motion quilting : go from simple to sensational with Sheila Sinclair Snyder / Sheila Sinclair Snyder.

  pages cm

 ISBN 978-1-60705-782-6 (soft cover)

 1. Patchwork--Patterns. 2. Machine quilting--Patterns. I. Title.

 TT835.S6193 2013

 746.46--dc23

2013002261

Printed in China

10 9 8 7 6 5 4 3 2 1

Dedication

This book is dedicated to my great friend Judy Dillree. She was the first person to encourage me to buy a longarm machine. She was the connection to some great quilt shops that began passing out my business cards and trusted me with their sample quilts. Judy has continued to make inspiring quilts, and her use of color melts me! I'd also like to mention some inspirational quilters who may not have been aware of their influence but who opened my eyes to the possibilities of machine quilting back in 1999 when I first started: Janet Fogg, Linda Taylor, Jodi Beamish, and Marilyn Badger—you still inspire me!

Acknowledgments

I am sometimes amazed to be surrounded by supportive people who encourage, inspire, and take away distractions when I am buried in deadlines. Once again my family took up the torch of cooking and cleaning so I could concentrate. To Julia and Spencer, Matthew and Samantha, *you* are my inspiration. You bring so much love, beauty, humor, and energy to my life. I can't imagine not taking every step with you. To my husband, Elvin, *you* are my hero! So capable, sensible, and caring for 36 years, and I'm looking forward to more!

I've had the help of my little quilt group too. Meeting deadlines can be tricky, as there is such a volume of work to be done. Carol, Yolaine, Margaret, Arlene, Sandy, Viki, Marcia, Lela, Ruth, and my dependable neighbor Marie helped with making blocks, binding, and labels as I was speeding toward a deadline. They are generous with their time and talents even though they could easily give me the boot, since I only occasionally have time to meet in person with them!

I've had the support of Lynn Koolish, Gailen Runge, Roxanne Cerda, Joanna Burgarino, Doreen Hazel, and Valyrie Friedman, who all trusted me and helped prepare this book. The book designer, Rose Wright, and the photographers, Diane Pedersen and Mary Peyton Peppo, made everything clear and beautiful.

Thank you so much. I truly appreciate all you have done.

Contents

INTRODUCTION 6

THE PROCESS 8

    Supplies • Choosing designs • Color options • Your license to quilt

Quilt as Inspired: Quilting Designs 13

SPRINGY THINGS 14

SPURS 18

BLOSSOM 22

SWOOSH AND SWIRL 26

M&M'S 30

CONTINUOUS CURVE 34

BREEZY MAPLE LEAVES 38

MASCULINE DESIGNS: POISON IVY AND SUNSHINE 42

ASIAN 46

TOPOGRAPHIC 50

FEATHER PLAY 54

Project: The Studio Quilt 60

ABOUT THE AUTHOR 63

Introduction

Free-motion quilting can be accomplished many ways: using a home sewing machine or a shortarm, midarm, or longarm quilting machine. I feel lucky to have a longarm machine that I am as comfortable with as if it were an extension of me. It was a different story when I started in 1999. But it doesn't take long to learn something new when you immerse yourself in it full-time. Now, I feel like I can quilt much better than I can draw, and that's directly correlated to how much I do of each.

I've chosen my most original and unique designs for this book. Many of them have evolved over the years from the original few designs I learned when I began quilting. Every design starts as a simple pattern. As I develop some expertise with it, I will begin to think about how it can be embellished and modified to suit other quilts.

Most designs can also be used in a variety of scales, such as a medium-to-large allover design or a small-to-micro background fill. I also imagine how some part of it might be used as a border or sashing. The combination may or may not be used on the same quilt, but having so many options for using a design that I already know builds the repertoire I have at my disposal.

Quilt designs have a progression and evolution—each design starts with a basic rendition, then it is modified once or twice to create more complicated designs, and, finally, border and sashing techniques are added. I tend to think about the progression as a series of levels:

1. Interested

2. Involved

3. Addicted!

Addicted!—Ha-ha! That's me all right! It's not a gradual development. It's full speed ahead. I like to push myself and my students to the next level. So throughout the book, look for the progressions and the added sashing and border designs. I hope you'll find some fun new inspirations.

Interested

Involved

Addicted!

The Process

Supplies

Quilters have stuff! We are drawn to checking out any new gadget that comes along. Who could deny the advancements that technology and innovation have brought to the industry? So bring it on, all you manufacturers, inventors, and distributors. We'll test it, use it, collect it, and look forward to the next new thing.

As a longarm quilter I have an arsenal of tools that are must-haves for me. Space is number one on the list—I need lots of space for my longarm machine. And for those of you who quilt on midarm or home machines, you also need space, especially surface space, so your quilts don't drag off the quilting table. We all need storage space for batting, quilt tops waiting to be quilted, and, of course, thread. We also need a big bookshelf to hold our quilting books and patterns. Great lighting means your eyes won't be strained after quilting for many hours. Mostly I use full-spectrum overhead lights, but sometimes it's necessary to use backlights or side lights, and once in a while I like to quilt with no lights at all, just the daylight coming in the window.

The tools I use at the machine are not limited to these, but they're definitely among my favorites:

- Antifatigue mats for the floor at both the front and back of the machine (for stand-up quilting, such as at a longarm)
- A straightedge as a guide for fussy things such as straight lines
- Marking tools
- Circle templates—I use them for marking only.
- Thread of every color—solids, variegated, and specialty threads. If you haven't tried metallic thread on velvet, you are in for a treat!
- I have my favorite seam ripper—not that I have to use it much, but there are those times. It has a flat handle so it won't roll off the quilt.
- The little curved scissors I use to snip thread are indispensable. They fit my hand perfectly and are very sharp and pointed. Of course, I also have good shears for trimming batting.

Choosing Designs

Choosing the quilting design for any given quilt is a very personal undertaking. There are always great options. I like to unfold the quilt and look at it for a while, and then think about it while I'm loading it onto the machine. Sometimes I load it the night before I'll be working on it, and that gives me some time to consider the options. In general I will do whatever the quilt needs, whether it takes two hours or twenty. Sometimes there's a deadline, and sometimes the customer will set a dollar amount for quilting, so the choices become more limited. Of course, if you are quilting your own quilts you can take as much time as you want.

I've been lucky to have quilted more than 3,000 quilts and have streamlined the process of deciding what to quilt. I start by getting a sense of the personality of the quilt and how it will be used. That helps me decide whether it needs to be loosely or closely quilted.

Loosely Spaced Quilting

A quilt that I might choose to quilt in an allover design with a loosely spaced motif would be a simply pieced cotton, flannel, or wool quilt. It might also be a very blended quilt—one that has intricate piecing but with an indistinct design and lots of scrappy fabrics or a blended background that camouflages the block.

Loose quilting, with ½"–1" (or more) spacing between the lines, will preserve the loft of the fabric and the batting. I love wool batting for these quilts

Quilt by Barbara Kimberley. Shown at Pacific Northwest Quilt Expo, Portland, Oregon, 2012.

because of the higher loft and dimension it provides. The quilt becomes the soft, cuddly, "curl up with a book" quilt, or the "take it with you camping" quilt. In fact, I'm picturing a lazy Sunday afternoon nap quilt right now!

Closely Spaced Quilting

I consider quilting lines that are spaced from $\frac{1}{16}$" to $\frac{3}{8}$" apart as closely spaced quilting. Quilts I would choose to quilt with a closely spaced design have distinct blocks, intricate piecing, or open spaces to show the quilting. They might be art quilts or quilted projects such as bags and purses. This type of quilting is fun to do, and the results make it worth the effort and extra time it takes.

Combination of Loosely and Closely Spaced Quilting

There are times when I think it's perfectly acceptable to use a combination of closely spaced quilting and loosely spaced quilting in the same quilt. Some people think that it is important to maintain the same quilting density over the entire quilt. That is true to a degree for an allover design, although even then I like to vary the size and shape of the designs just to make the quilting more interesting.

By the way, have I mentioned that I especially love a hand-guided folk-art look? If I wanted perfection I would get a computerized machine. What I want is the artistic quality that comes from being able to "draw" the quilting onto the quilt. So, when I use closely spaced quilting along with loosely spaced quilting, for me it compares to using large-scale prints with small-scale prints or solids—it enriches the design and makes it more interesting.

When you see a quilt from a distance, at a quilt show, for example, and it catches your eye, you might say to yourself, "Oh, I've got to see that one up close." Later you come around a corner and are captivated enough to stay and study it. You realize it's the many layers of design that make it a great quilt. The quilting becomes the icing on the cake, finishing the design and creating more interest and movement than was visible at a distance. That is one of the treasures of quilting.

Many layers of design

Photo by Sheila Sinclair Snyder

Color Options

When I first started quilting for other people, I had only a handful of designs that I felt I could execute well enough to charge for, and I wasn't a very confident quilter. Looking back, I am so grateful for those customers from my first year. They really went out on a limb! They trusted me with their work, and it was a big responsibility. I started out using mostly neutral threads, afraid that imperfections would be so glaringly obvious that I would never get any repeat customers.

Of course, now I'm very bold with thread choices, color, and fibers. It's a different ball game. I realized early on that quilting isn't just a way to stitch the quilt layers together. It is a layer of design in itself. I choose thread color as carefully as I choose fabric, auditioning many options. Sometimes a quilt will need a more neutral thread that will allow the dimension of the quilting to show off the piecing. Sometimes a quilt will need a punch of color to continue its story.

I like to choose the thread color after I have the quilt loaded onto the machine. It gives me a flat surface on which to evaluate each thread. I grab several spools from my rack and toss out a strand of thread from each of the selected spools onto the quilt so it gently loops and flows over several different fabrics. Generally I can quickly eliminate some choices and put them away. It's not always the color I thought was obvious that ends up in the quilt. As my tastes have changed and evolved over the years, I'm using fewer neutrals and having a lot more fun!

Photo by Tom Urich, Urich Photography

Your License to Quilt

Go forth and quilt!

Try out the designs in this book, develop your own variations, and expand your quilting repertoire. I always tell my students: "It's not that I think you should quilt just like me. Even if you tried, there would be a difference. I know you will take these designs and make them your own—give them your signature and personality. The designs will evolve as you perfect each one."

It takes practice to develop the confidence to choose a design that enhances each quilt, pick thread colors that continue the story of each quilt, and have the energy and desire to complete each quilt.

Many quilts require thread color changes. I am happy to change thread as many times as it takes. When I need to change colors, I do it as I complete each section of the quilt; then I roll the quilt forward and repeat the same colors. Some quilters complete one thread color at a time for the whole quilt, and I will do this for small pieces. But in a large quilt that isn't completely stabilized, rolling it back and forth to add another thread color runs the risk of stitching a pleat here and there on the back, and sometimes even on the front of the quilt. The fabrics and the batting can shift a bit (enough to cause problems), so I stick to my method of completing each section as I go, even if it means changing thread colors a billion times. You will find the method that works best for you.

Quilt. Be *happy*. Have a *good* life. Create *beauty!*

The Process 11

Quilt as

Inspired

Springy Things

Use these springy designs in every scale. When the arcs face in different directions, they have more interest and energy. It's a playful design, so try it on whimsical, juvenile, art, and ethnic quilts.

Interested

Start with a spiral with a point in the center. It turns into a coil that is echoed in arcs to arrive at a new location to begin again.

Involved

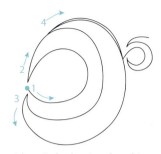

Go with a circle that is echoed in arcs. Partially retrace the last arc to travel to a new location for the next motif. Use different sizes of the motif to give this design even more dimension and texture.

Addicted!

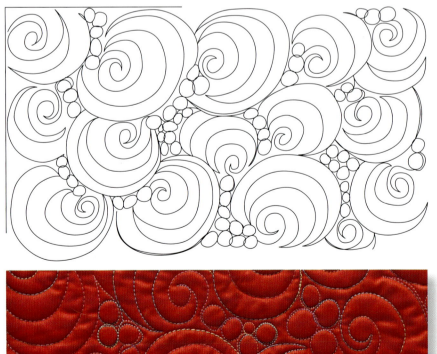

Begin with a coil; then use a line or cluster of small circles to travel to a new place to begin again. Each circle is retraced to get to the start of the next circle in the chain. The design can be very regular or wildly varied, depending on your taste and what the quilt needs.

Borders and Sashing

Don't you love these springy borders? They have so much energy. Use them in every size, on any type of quilt. Come up with your own combinations. Springy Things are a never-ending source of border ideas!

Spurs

Spurs are another progression of springs—very playful and fun to stitch. Notice how they morph from straight to curvy. Echo the designs to give them more visibility and prominence on the quilt.

Interested

Start with a coil, then stitch a big zigzag line around the coil and echo back, or head to a new place to begin again with a coil. The goal is to have the zigzags arcing in random directions across the space. Notice that the starting point is far enough down on the left side to give you enough space above it to make the first spur.

Involved

Use a divide-and-conquer method by choosing a portion of a motif, in this case spurs, and developing a new design from it. The diagonal lines of this design will draw the eye to different areas of the quilt. Try shifting to a new diagonal for another look.

Addicted!

The spurs, with curves! Wow!

Borders and Sashing

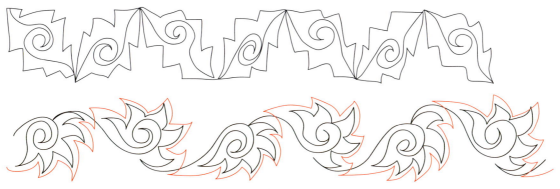

Talk about wow borders! Notice the second line (in red) that echoes the trailing spurs, giving it a lot more dimension than it would otherwise have had.

This is the border design used on my friend Barbara Kimberley's quilt (page 9). Try it in a large (6″ or wider) border: Fill each side of the border with a different background quilting design to really give it that WOW factor.

Designer TIP *This is the first of many three-part motifs. The first line (the centerline) starts at the left and moves to the right, ending at what will become the starting point for the next motif. The second line goes over the top and back to the left, forming the upper part of the motif. The third line moves to the right, forming the lower part of the motif. And then you're ready to start with the centerline of the next motif.*

Blossom

Blossom is a very curvy and feminine design. Embellish it with swirls, echoing, and circles, depending on the density you want. It is sometimes a challenge to twist and turn this design so that the blossoms face in random directions, so keep that in mind. Use the echo and the direction you start the petals to help change the look of the blossom.

Interested

The smooth and flowing look of this folk-art blossom may seem different from those that follow, but it is made following the same idea of a central core surrounded by petals, then echoed to a place to begin again. The beginning swirl has a curved center that gives it a softer look on the quilt. The petals have a rounded outside edge and a narrow neck—no sharp points anywhere. Begin by making the swirl and then surrounding it with petals. The number of petals used is dependent on the space available.

Involved

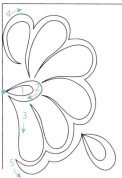

Start at the left edge of the quilt by making a teardrop. Echo it once and begin "blossoming" from one side of the teardrop to the other. Long tapering petals give this design a graceful look. Echo back to the beginning edge to start again. You will sometimes need to echo a short distance to travel to a new beginning spot. If needed, use swirls to fill an awkward space or to travel to a new beginning.

Addicted!

Add small circles to the blossom for a totally different look. Instead of echoing, use the circles to travel to a new place to begin another blossom. Quilting the background heavily and uniformly gives the blossom the look of trapunto.

24   Get Addicted to Free-Motion Quilting

Borders and Sashing

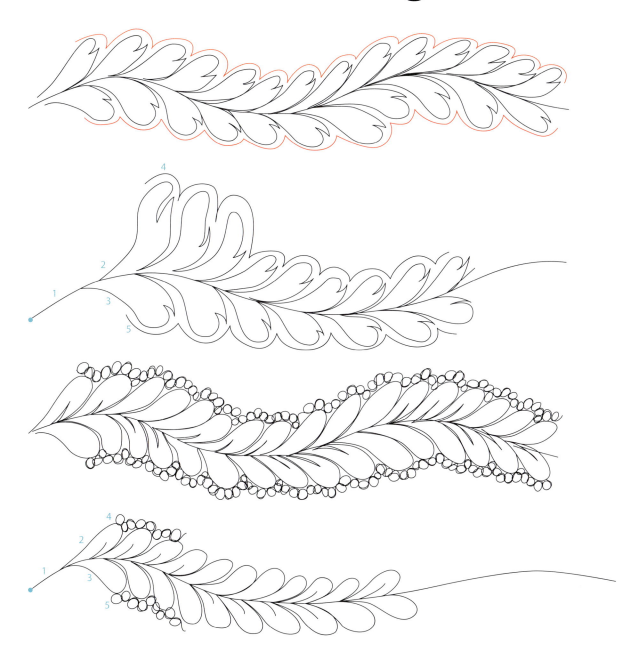

Blossoms turn into feathers for borders. Change the shape of the feather as well as how it is echoed. Think about changing the color of the echo. Echoing in a colored thread enlarges the design, while using a neutral background color will define the feather and give it more texture.

These designs are each made up of five independent lines. All start at the left: (1) centerline, (2) upper curves of the petals, (3) lower curves of the petals, (4) upper echo or bubbles, and finally (5) lower echo or bubbles.

Swoosh and Swirl

Swoosh and Swirl is a wonderful flowing design. It echoes back and forth to travel between swirls that are placed at random intervals. I started adding some little zigzags to create more interest and to give the design some angles rather than more curves. From there it was an easy leap to adding floral motifs, as you will see. Begin by learning this design in a medium scale. After that it is easy to switch to a mini or large scale to suit your quilt.

Interested

Begin at the edge of the quilt with a swirl, branch off with some swooshes, and then echo back and forth to a new location to make another swirl. Change directions frequently as you spread the design across the quilt. Add in some zigzags with echoes here and there to give the design lots of angles and interest.

Involved

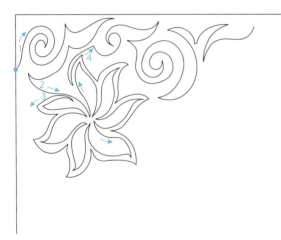

The Floral Meander uses the basic Swoosh and Swirl design to travel around the quilt and to add motifs along the way. The motifs I use are flowers, leaves, clusters of flowers, and even a few fruits and vegetables. To help me decide on the next motif to include, I have a cheat sheet prepared of all the motifs I want to use so I can glance at them as I'm traveling with the Swoosh and Swirl. Notice that the motifs are generally echoed to make them more visible. If the flowers are small, I make them into a cluster and echo them as a group rather than individually. (The red lines shown here are just to help you see the floral motifs more easily.)

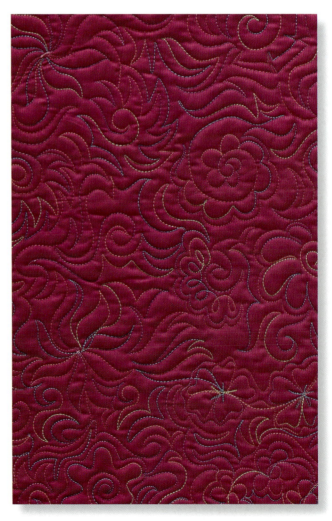

Addicted!

The more addicted you get, the more motifs you'll want to add. You may already know some flowers and other motifs, but here are some fun ones to add to the mix. See if you can figure out the stitching sequence. Then try your own variations— the possibilities are endless!

Swoosh and Swirl

M&M's

What a fun and easily modified design! The angles of the M's contrast with the softness of the loops, making it neither masculine nor feminine. The best effect is to alter the angle at which the M's are stitched so that instead of lining up in rows they fall at irregular angles. This gives the design more interest and draws the eye across the quilt. You can see how easy it is to draw these out into a line for a border or sashing, so don't forget about using them in that way too.

Interested

Straight M&M's are fast and easy—they are simply alternating zigzags and loops. Alter the direction of the M's to keep the look on the quilt very random and spontaneous, and use the loops to travel. Changing the number of loops, the orientation (faceup or facedown), and the spacing will also help you travel to a new position on the quilt.

Involved

Curved M&M's are also stitched with alternating loops, but here the zigzags can spring out in different directions, giving the design an interesting, active effect.

Addicted!

Ribbon M&M's look like they would take twice as much time as the original M&M's, but in fact they take only a bit longer. The thought and planning of fitting the design into the space takes place on the first thread. You start at the left with one line swirling to the right across the quilt. Then, without stopping, echo or ribbon backward along the original line. The idea is not to trace but to echo, crossing lines and leaving small spaces between the first and second lines. When you add a second line, the design becomes much more visible and has a more substantial presence on the quilt.

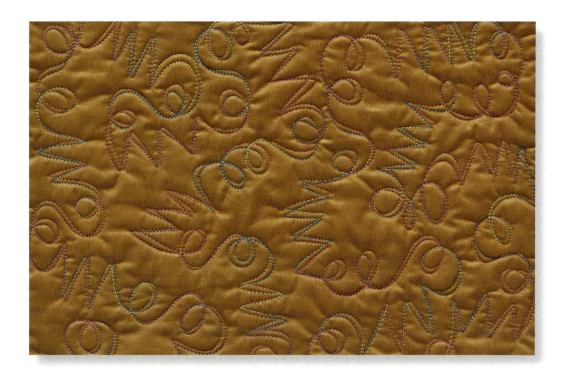

Borders and Sashing

Run lines of zigzags and loops for borders and sashing. For extra emphasis, echo the lines.

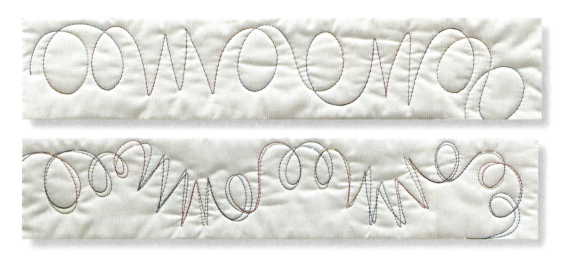

Continuous Curve

Continuous Curve is a great approach for quilting blocks. If you alter the simple, basic curve and give it some flare as it travels, you will see that it looks much more complicated, even though it is built on the original Continuous Curve.

One mistake many quilters make as they are learning this design relates to the speed. Going slow, for perfection, actually makes it harder to get a nice curve into the corners. So practice picking up the speed, allowing your eyes to bounce from corner to corner. That will help your body move more smoothly.

Interested

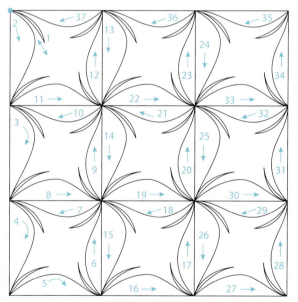

To make the design, start by making a short "flag" in the direction you will travel for the Continuous Curve and trace backward to the starting point. Then make a generous curve under the flag, and taper into the next corner. Or you can choose to make the curve over the flag to enclose it. Watch the pinwheel develop as you complete each section. Only touch the seams at the intersections!

Involved

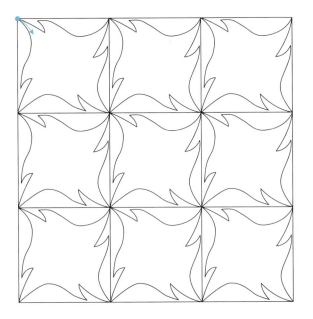

For this variation, begin in the upper left corner by stitching an arc down toward the next intersection. Then make a backwards zigzag before continuing down to touch the intersection. Follow the diagram on page 35 for the stitching sequence. The repeated motions of Continuous Curve designs make it easy to get into a rhythm with your body that lends itself to quilting very methodically. This gives the quilting a nicely uniform and harmonious look.

The effect on the quilt is so fun—depending on the thread you choose. Can you see the seahorse? It might be fun to try on a blue batik. I planned this design by embellishing the outside of the curve.

Addicted!

Oh, boy, we're having fun now! I call this version the Hurricane Continuous Curve (it's my favorite). I use it on larger blocks because it is more complicated and shows more thread. Sometimes I even echo it in the center—just because I can. Think about that generous curve bumping up into the block to begin, but you're actually stitching a swirl. Zigzag twice, getting smaller, and then dive down into the second corner. That's how it goes—round and round. I've used this as a large-scale motif to fill open spaces on my quilts. By adding a small background fill around the outside, as well as inside the motif, you'll create a sort of faux trapunto design.

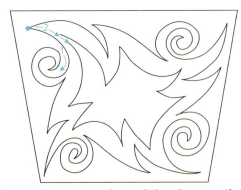

Using the Hurricane as a single stand-alone large motif, you can morph it to any geometric shape. Echo the design by simply following the curves and zigzags as you travel around the inside edge of stitching.

Over the Top Freehand Cable

What describes a continuous curve more than a cable? I like to make cables freehand, with all the irregularity and wonkiness that happens with freehand. The corners can be challenging to think your way through, but planning, and possibly doing some marking, will help. After some practice they are very manageable. Use the seamlines for spacing or mark chalk lines in regular intervals—this will help with spacing as you are learning this design.

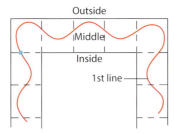

The first line starts in the upper left; arc around the outer edge of the corner, traveling to the right. Stitch in arcs to the opposite corner—that will also be part of the outer edge. The outward arcs will graze to within ¼"–½" of the outside edge of the border. The inward arcs will drop to just below the imaginary centerline of the border.

If you are quilting on a longarm machine, travel down the right border as far as you can before stopping. Returning to the start, begin in the same stitch and travel down the left border as far as you can. If you are using a domestic machine, you should be able to go all the way around the quilt with one pass per stitched line.

Burying your thread tails will help hide any stops and starts. After you have some experience you will be able to stitch all four lines without marking.

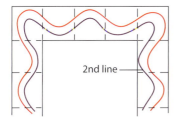

The second line echoes but does not cross the first line. I like to exaggerate the curves a little and vary the space between the two lines. The second line should fall ¼"–½" away from the inside edge of the border.

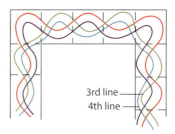

The third line is stitched in the same manner to fill the open space created by the curves of the first two lines. Note that this is the line that forms "shoulders" on each side of the corner. Once you have stitched the third line, it is easy to simply echo it to form a four-line cable.

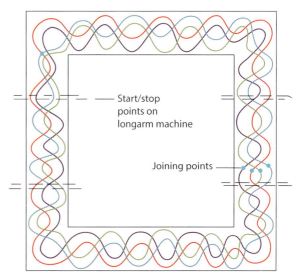

On a longarm machine you'll have multiple stops and starts. The number depends on the length of your quilt. Try to avoid having lines meet at the center of an arc—it's harder to make a smooth transition. When you are ready to join the last lines together (no matter what type of machine you use), take one stitch at a time by advancing the handwheel for the last inch or so in order to make a perfectly smooth transition. Then bury your threads for a nice finish.

Breezy Maple Leaves

Breezy Maple Leaves are not intended to be true to nature. The design is intended to be a very large-scale organic motif, a little more masculine than feminine. I sometimes make these leaves as big as plates. For example, it's great as an all-over design for a flannel quilt that doesn't need something more custom.

Interested

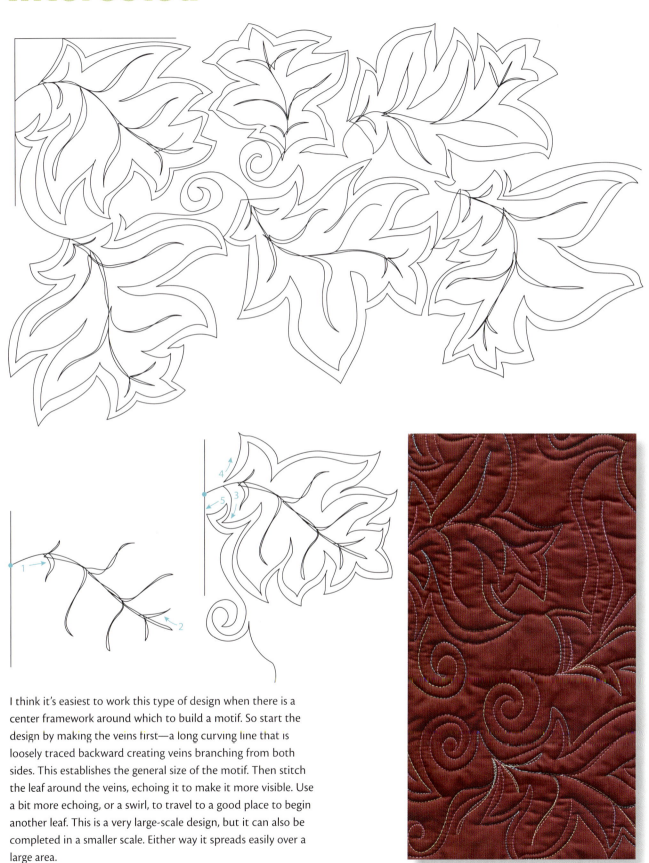

I think it's easiest to work this type of design when there is a center framework around which to build a motif. So start the design by making the veins first—a long curving line that is loosely traced backward creating veins branching from both sides. This establishes the general size of the motif. Then stitch the leaf around the veins, echoing it to make it more visible. Use a bit more echoing, or a swirl, to travel to a good place to begin another leaf. This is a very large-scale design, but it can also be completed in a smaller scale. Either way it spreads easily over a large area.

Breezy Maple Leaves

Involved

The Breezy Maple Leaf becomes an Oak Leaf! The motif can return to the stem end like the maple leaf (page 39), or you can make the leading edge the top of the leaf rather than the stem, and that makes it trail over the quilt differently.

Addicted!

To make the Breezy Maple Leaves (or Oak Leaves) more identifiable and visible, I like to use dense echo quilting as a background fill between the leaves. In the sample (pages 38 and 41) I used a variegated thread for the leaves and a solid coordinating-color thread for the background. It has the effect of changing the background color in a subtle way to emphasize the leaf—a fun effect!

Borders and Sashing

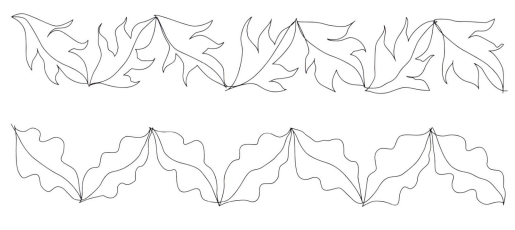

Why not use Breezy Maple or Oak Leaves in a border or sashing? They will begin at one edge and end at the opposite edge, making it easy to trail them in zigzag fashion around a border or to turn a corner in sashing. (See Designer Tip for three-part designs on page 21.) There are options for turning the corners, depending on whether you have an even number or odd number of motifs. I will often use both options in the same quilt, as that is simply how it works out. You may be able to use the pieced seams as a guide for the size of the motif, or you may choose to mark the quilt at regular intervals with chalk or a wash-away marker.

Masculine Designs:
Poison Ivy and Sunshine

There are a ton of feminine designs out there, but not so many masculine ones. I designed Poison Ivy for a flannel quilt I was making for my son. If the name bothers you, you can call it just plain Ivy! I like this design because once again you build the motif from a center framework, controlling the size and direction. But this one is different in how it spreads on the quilt. Instead of starting at the edge, you start in the middle of the space and work in a counterclockwise direction. This keeps the leaves twisting and turning for a very random look, like leaves tossed on the forest floor.

Interested

Start in the middle of your quilt, not at the edge. Make what I call a "bird track"—three lines spreading from a common point. Then swing out to make a leaf around each vein of the bird track without returning all the way to the center each time. Continue by echoing around the leaf to a new position to begin the second bird track.

Move in a counterclockwise direction so the leaves twist and turn each time. Adding a loop or two here and there will fill the awkward spaces not big enough to complete a leaf. You can also add a single leaf or a double leaf here and there for the same reason, especially around the edges. You will eventually need to tie off and restart in another section of the quilt. I usually have three or four stops and starts before the space is filled and I'm ready to roll the quilt forward.

Masculine Designs: Poison Ivy and Sunshine

Involved

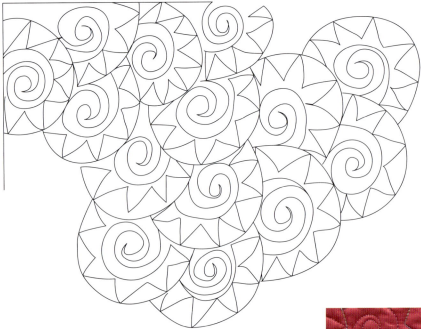

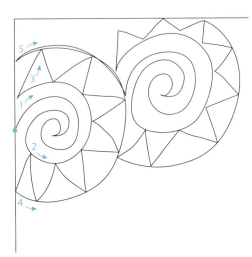

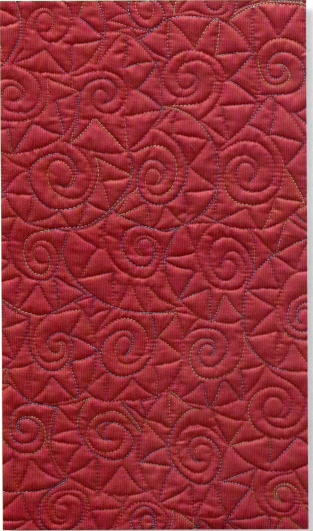

Sunshine is another masculine design. I also like it for whimsical or juvenile quilts. It's a fun one to stitch, and easier than it looks. Start with a swirl, circle around back to the beginning, and begin making zigzags in an arc around the swirl. Next make a final arc connecting the outer points of the zigzags. From there you can choose to begin again or travel to a new location by retracing the arc stitching. You think you won't be able to connect the points? Not so! Your body just made those points and somehow remembers where they are. Try not to look at each one, but concentrate on curving to the end.

Borders and Sashing

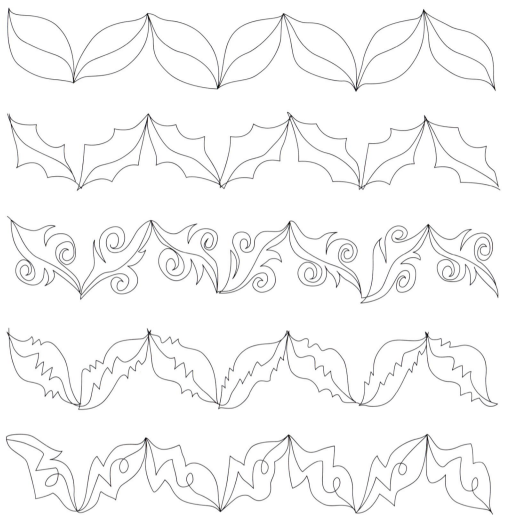

Three-part trailing leaves make for great masculine borders and sashing. Here are a few to try out and play with. I bet you'll come up with more of your own. (See Designer Tip for three-part designs on page 21.)

Asian

I love to see Asian quilts and quilting, but Asian design is not something that comes naturally to me. So as I was developing my longarm business, I needed to come up with some designs I could use for those quilts that came in only occasionally. I still use these designs. They are very basic and can be stitched around appliquéd motifs or hand sashiko, or used as allover designs as well.

Interested

Horizontal flowing water is a familiar Asian aesthetic. Keep this design very horizontal with curved turns. Staggering the turns and spacing while keeping the design very random feels the best. Try ribboning back with a very close echo on the horizontal lines and a looser echo on the turns. This is done only here and there on the design, not on every line.

Involved

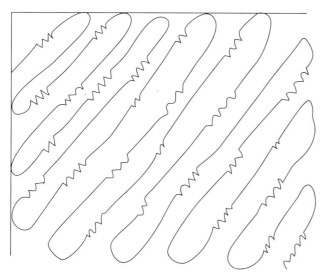

Turning the design on the diagonal (and adding some zigzags) is a good way to add movement and texture. You may need to chalk in some diagonal lines just to keep the angles straight. Especially if you want to make the design change direction, lines will help to keep you from getting what I call "lost in space"!

Addicted!

Start with the horizontal flowing water technique (page 47) and add a lotus blossom or other motif at random intervals. This can be done on the body of the quilt and also as a border treatment, wherever it will be visible. I use a lotus blossom cut from template plastic, which I roughly trace with chalk or a wash-away marker. After marking, begin stitching the horizontal flowing water as a background. When you come to the marked motif, stitch it and then continue by echoing back or traveling to the next motif. Audition gold, black, or red thread for a striking effect.

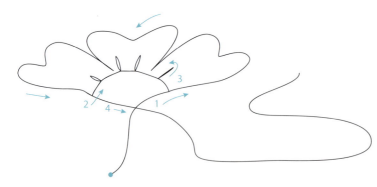

Start the lotus motif by stitching to the right as a continuation of one of the horizontal flowing water lines. Trace the petals as you move from right to left and then arc back to the right under the petals. Continue by retracing the center arc, adding definition to the petals as you go. Then move down to the bottom and cross the original line, and you're ready for more flowing water!

Borders and Sashing

The horizontal flowing water and lotus blossom technique is also very effective in borders and sashing. Echo the flowing water lines for greater impact.

Topographic

One of my all-time favorites, Topographic is versatile in scale, simplicity/complexity, and usefulness. I like it as an all-over design for large blended quilts without distinct blocks. Because of its organic nature it's great for landscape, water, wind, and sand. I use it in smaller bits for art quilts. In a larger scale it will keep the quilt very loose and flexible. In any scale it adds a lot of texture and dimension. The diagonals and the shift in diagonals help move the eye around the quilt.

You may not need a separate border treatment—just continue the design through any sashing and into the borders!

Interested

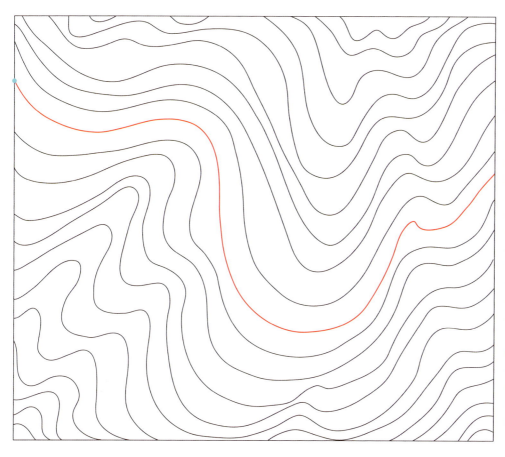

Start with a line (shown in red) that waves up and down across the middle of your quilting area so that you have space above and below the line to fill with additional lines. I stop and backstitch at the edge of the quilt for almost every line, unless it is a short line at the top or bottom of the quilt. Fill in the top of the quilt before you proceed past the original line. Loosely echo the lines as you stitch. I don't try to make spaces perfectly even; it's more interesting if they are staggered. Finish the bottom of the quilt in the same way. You will need to fill in with some shorter lines along the top and bottom edges of the quilt.

> " The first time I used this design was for my dear friend Judy. She just about fell over backward in love! I hadn't used anything but exaggerated wavy lines. It really looked like a topographical map, and she was thrilled. I was too."

Involved

Add a swirl in the concave sections, making the wave change direction under the swirls. Add swirls randomly for a more organic effect.

Addicted!

Add swirls, short or long lines of circles, clusters of circles, hurricanes, and other organic shapes into the topographic waves. Exaggerate the shape and density of the waves for even more excitement!

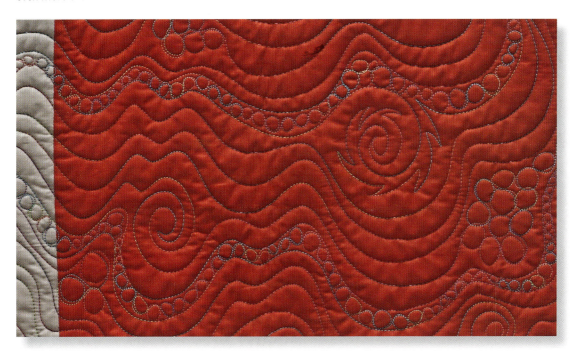

Feather Play

Feathers have been a standard in quilting design for as long as people have quilted. They add grace and polish. I doubt they will ever go out of style. They have changed and evolved over the years, especially with the advent of machine quilting.

Feathers can easily be adapted to any scale or any space. The texture that is added has uniformity to it, but also a bit of randomness. So it has interest from a distance and close up—both in overall designs and in wreaths. I've enjoyed developing many feathered wreaths over the years—some have a more traditional feathered look, and some are feather-inspired. You will notice that of the feathered wreaths included, two are densely quilted in the background. This background quilting helps identify and highlight the wreath. One design is intentionally left with an unquilted background so you can see what that looks like.

The choice is yours. Do what the quilt needs, following the guidelines required for the batting. Most of all, have fun!

Interested

This basic allover feather design is a gently curving design with many of the feathers curling into each other. You can see how easily you could spread this large-scale design across an entire quilt.

Start with the centerline—it defines the length and curve of the feather. Loop to make the first feather "petal" at the top and then continue down one side, making feather petals as you go. Cross the centerline and feather the other side to the top. Retrace the centerline back to the start. Echo the entire design and swirl your way to a new location and the next feather.

When you are comfortable with the design, be sure to try it in a smaller scale. The added swirls are used to travel to a new space and to spread the motifs apart so they become more visible. I tend to echo each motif as I go, emphasizing each feather so it stands out more. I also often use a thread color that gives it some punch. For a softer look, simply omit the echo and choose a thread that blends with the fabrics.

Feather Play

Involved

Feathers lend themselves easily to wreaths that can be used as block designs for plain or pieced blocks. This one is a variation of the traditional feathered wreath, using two feather motifs. After stitching the wreath itself, decide whether or not to quilt the background. Notice that I chose a different color for the background quilting to make the feathered wreath even more prominent. (See stitched sample below.) I always try to choose something really different for the background, as that will show off the motif best.

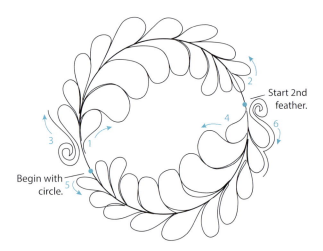

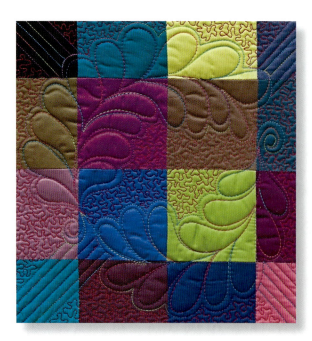

Mark the quilt to give yourself a target area. Begin stitching the circle and then lead into a feather. The second feather is a new start, stitched as a separate motif.

Addicted!

Start with circle.

Inside edge of circle

This is a fun feathered wreath that combines several ideas—curls, bubbles, arcs, and echoes.

Though there are many design elements here, the stitching sequence for this wreath is simpler than it appears. Mark the original circle and the outside edge to keep the size of each element consistent as you stitch. Start by stitching the circle and then proceed to the feather motifs on the inside edge. Once you've completed the inside motifs, continue stitching around the circle to make the outside-edge feather motifs. You'll need more motifs on the outside edge, so don't be surprised! To continue, start again by arcing around the outside edge and over each feather motif. As you stitch the arcs a second time, add a simple sprouting element at each crevice. This wreath can easily have an added background, but I wanted you to see what it would look like plain. In some cases you might prefer this simpler look.

Feather Play

More Addiction

This feather-inspired wreath may look familiar! It's the Springy Things border variation (page 59) adapted to make a stylized feather circling into a wreath. Practice by drawing this on paper first, and you will see how easy it is. I love the convoluted outside edge of this design and the way the wreath becomes a leafy design when the outside echo is added. The background is densely quilted with variable textures that rotate in each quadrant to give maximum interest.

Start with circle.

Stitch inner motifs around circle first, then stitch outer motifs.

To stitch, mark a large circle and divide the space into an even number of sections (I used six in this sample). That gives you a target for the spiral that begins each motif on the inside. It is easy to stitch the outside edge, lining up the spirals and tapering the arcs to finish the motif. Use as many arcs as needed to fill the space—typically more than needed on the inside curve. When the last motif is finished, echo the whole wreath as a unit on both the inside and outside edges. This defines the motif and also gives an edge for the background quilting.

Borders and Sashing

Let's not forget the beautiful natural feather that inspired all the feathering designs from the beginning. I love to use trailing designs in borders and sashing, and the options are endless for building a design around the gently waving line in the center of the space.

Stitch the center wave first as a separate line. Begin again at the starting point with a few little spikes for the downy portion that identifies the beginning of the feather. Continue on to create one edge of the feather (count the number of divots to keep them consistent), meet the line in a point, and stitch back to the beginning, creating the opposite edge of the feather. Follow the wavy line, crossing over it as you stitch, beyond the tip of the feather to begin again. Remember that real-life feathers come in all sorts of shapes and sizes—thick, thin, long, or short—so use what's right for your quilt and the space available.

The second feathering design is another version of the Springy Things design (page 17). It's a good example of a trailing design that is stitched around a wavy line. Note that each line is stitched separately. It has a contemporary feeling, and is quite graceful and appealing. This time it is not echoed. Without a crisp edge the design stands out on its own and has a more free-form look.

The Studio Quilt

Finished block: 15″ × 15″ • **Finished quilt:** 75″ × 90″

Simple cutting and piecing and large blocks make this the perfect last-minute gift. Big blocks are a time-saver when it comes to piecing a quilt, and you'll have it ready to quilt before you know it. Show off your quilting in the large plain blocks and throw in some border and sashing elements, or try out an allover design (or more!) as I did in the sample.

The Michael Miller Cotton Couture fabrics I chose have a bit of sheen on one side that makes for some interesting effects in lamplight. I love the rich saturated colors and how they interact with each other, but other palettes will work equally well. Think about a "sun-washed end-of-the-summer" palette—yum!

Materials

Yardage is based on 42"-wide fabric.

Plain blocks: 15 fat quarters in a variety of solid colors (or 4 yards of a single fabric)

Pieced blocks: 2⅛ yards total in a variety of solid colors

The scraps need to be at least 3½" × 3½". A wide variety of fabrics is needed to achieve a scrappy effect.

Sashing: 1½ yards gray or white solid

Binding: ¾ yard

Backing: 5½ yards

Batting: 79" × 94"

Cutting Instructions

From solid fabric for plain blocks

Cut 1 square 15½" × 15½" from each fat quarter. Or cut 15 squares 15½" × 15½" from a single fabric.

From solid fabric for pieced blocks

Cut 1 strip 3½" × width of fabric for each color. Subcut the strips into squares 3½" × 3½". Each strip will make 12 squares. You need a total of 240 squares.

From sashing fabric

Cut 13 strips 3½" × width of fabric. Subcut the strips into 15 rectangles 3½" × 12½" and 15 rectangles 3½" × 15½".

From binding fabric

Cut 9 strips 2½" × width of fabric.

Block Assembly

Seam allowances are ¼". For the pieced portion of the block, press the seam allowances open.

 TIP *I generally choose a method of pressing that suits each quilt. My preference for this quilt is to press the seams open until adding the sashing in order to keep the seam allowances very flat and smooth. This allows me to use the pieced surface as a gridded palette for the quilting. Or by ignoring the seamlines, I can use it as a plain background for quilting. Pressing the seams open also helps maintain the true size of the block since the pressing doesn't take up any extra fabric.*

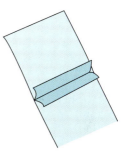

Press seams open.

1. For each pieced block, choose 16 squares 3½" × 3½" in a variety of colors. Place them in 4 rows of 4 squares. Sew together the squares into rows. Press the seams open. Sew together the rows into a 12½" × 12½" unit. Press the seams open.

Make 15.

The Studio Quilt 61

2. Sew a 3½˝ × 12½˝ sashing rectangle to the right side of each pieced block. Press the seam allowances toward the sashing.

3. Sew a 3½˝ × 15½˝ sashing rectangle to the bottom of each pieced block. Press the seam allowances toward the sashing.

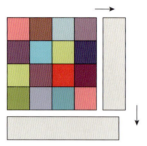

Make 15.

 If you are using white as your sashing color, I suggest you press the sashing seam allowances toward the pieced block. This will eliminate any possibility of the darker fabrics shadowing through the sashing. As you are quilting you'll also need to look carefully for any loose thread tails that might land behind the white fabric. They are extremely difficult to remove after quilting.

Quilt Construction

Refer to the quilt photo (page 60) and to the quilt assembly diagram (right). Follow the arrows for pressing direction.

1. Arrange the blocks, alternating pieced and plain blocks, in 6 rows of 5 blocks each.

2. Sew the blocks into rows. Press the seam allowances in opposite directions from row to row, so the seams will nest when you sew together the rows.

3. Sew together the rows. Press the seam allowances all in one direction.

Finishing the Quilt

1. Cut the backing fabric into 2 equal lengths of 94˝. Trim off the selvage edges. Sew the pieces together lengthwise to make a large piece at least 79˝ × 94˝. If you are using a longarm quilting machine, you may want to add extra length to both the batting and backing.

2. Layer and baste.

3. Quilt as inspired! The sample quilt was quilted using a few designs over large portions of the quilt. Using multiple quilting designs will give your quilt more interest and movement, as well as texture.

For a more custom option, take advantage of the sashing areas and quilt each area with a different motif. Changing thread colors is fun too!

Next, choose a different background design to fill in the diagonal lines of colorful blocks. Throw in some interesting continuous curves, and you will have a showstopper!

4. Prepare and attach the binding and label. You can find detailed instructions for bindings and labels on my website, licensetoquilt.com, or at tinyurl.com/quiltmaking-basics, or use your own favorite techniques.

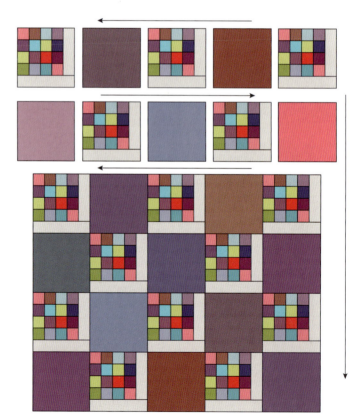

Quilt assembly diagram

62   Get Addicted to Free-Motion Quilting

About the Author

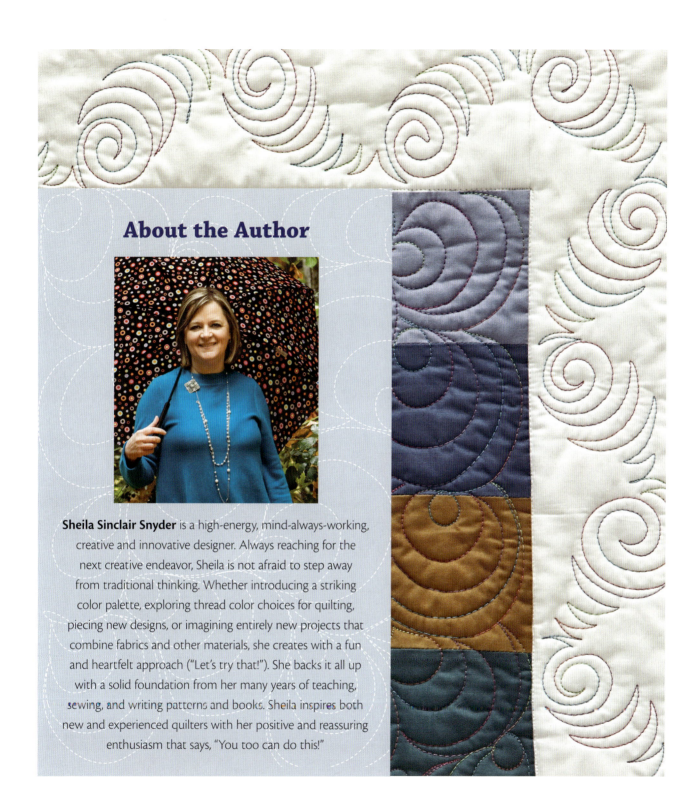

Sheila Sinclair Snyder is a high-energy, mind-always-working, creative and innovative designer. Always reaching for the next creative endeavor, Sheila is not afraid to step away from traditional thinking. Whether introducing a striking color palette, exploring thread color choices for quilting, piecing new designs, or imagining entirely new projects that combine fabrics and other materials, she creates with a fun and heartfelt approach ("Let's try that!"). She backs it all up with a solid foundation from her many years of teaching, sewing, and writing patterns and books. Sheila inspires both new and experienced quilters with her positive and reassuring enthusiasm that says, "You too can do this!"

Great Titles *from* C&T PUBLISHING

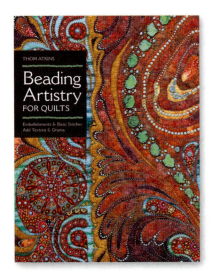
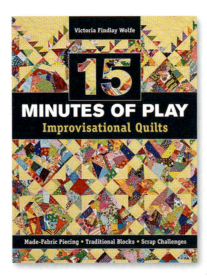
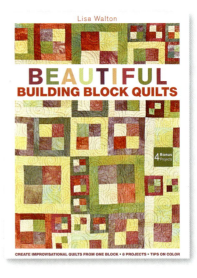

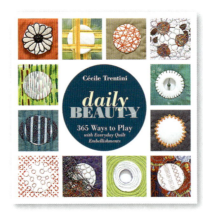
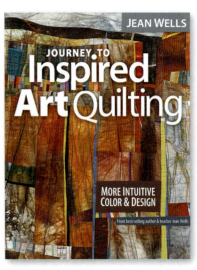

Available at your local retailer or **www.ctpub.com** or **800-284-1114**

For a list of other fine books from C&T Publishing, visit our website to view our catalog online.

C&T PUBLISHING, INC.
P.O. Box 1456
Lafayette, CA 94549
800-284-1114

Email: ctinfo@ctpub.com
Website: www.ctpub.com

C&T Publishing's professional photography services are now available to the public. Visit us at www.ctmediaservices.com.

Tips and Techniques can be found at www.ctpub.com > Consumer Resources > Quiltmaking Basics: Tips & Techniques for Quiltmaking & More

For quilting supplies:

COTTON PATCH
1025 Brown Ave.
Lafayette, CA 94549
Store: 925-284-1177
Mail order: 925-283-7883

Email: CottonPa@aol.com
Website: www.quiltusa.com

Note: Fabrics shown may not be currently available, as fabric manufacturers keep most fabrics in print for only a short time.